THE MORGAN HORSE

By Sara Green

Consultant:
Dr. Emily Leuthner
DVM, MS, DACVIM
Country View Veterinary Service
Oregon, Wisc.

BELLWETHER MEDIA • MINNEAPOLIS, MN

Jump into the cockpit and take flight with Pilot Books. Your journey will take you on high-energy adventures as you learn about all that is wild, weird, fascinating, and fun!

This edition first published in 2012 by Bellwether Media, Inc.

No part of this publication may be reproduced in whole or in part without written permission of the publisher. For information regarding permission, write to Bellwether Media, Inc., Attention: Permissions Department, 5357 Penn Avenue South, Minneapolis, MN 55419.

Library of Congress Cataloging-in-Publication Data

Green, Sara, 1964-
The Morgan horse / by Sara Green.
    p. cm. – (Pilot books. Horse breed roundup)
Includes bibliographical references and index.
Summary: "Engaging images accompany information about the Morgan horse. The combination of high-interest subject matter and narrative text is intended for students in grades 3 through 7"–Provided by publisher.
ISBN 978-1-60014-739-5 (hardcover : alk. paper)
1. Morgan horse–Juvenile literature. I. Title.
SF293.M8G74 2012
636.1'77–dc23   2011029433

Printed in the United States of America, North Mankato, MN.

010112   1204

CONTENTS

The Morgan Horse

The Morgan horses and their riders are excited to begin the marathon, the second round of the **combined driving** competition. Excited spectators line the 9-mile (15-kilometer) course to watch teams of Morgans pull carts in a race against the clock. The final stretch of the marathon includes a wide creek. The crowd cheers as the Morgans splash into and power through the water!

The Morgan horse is an intelligent breed with a calm **temperament**. Morgans are known for their willingness to work hard. People have used Morgans for difficult tasks for over 200 years. Morgans are also playful. They excel in a wide variety of fun horse activities. Their strength and **cooperative** spirit help them succeed on the racetrack, in the **show ring**, and on the riding trail. Work or play, the Morgan is happy to participate.

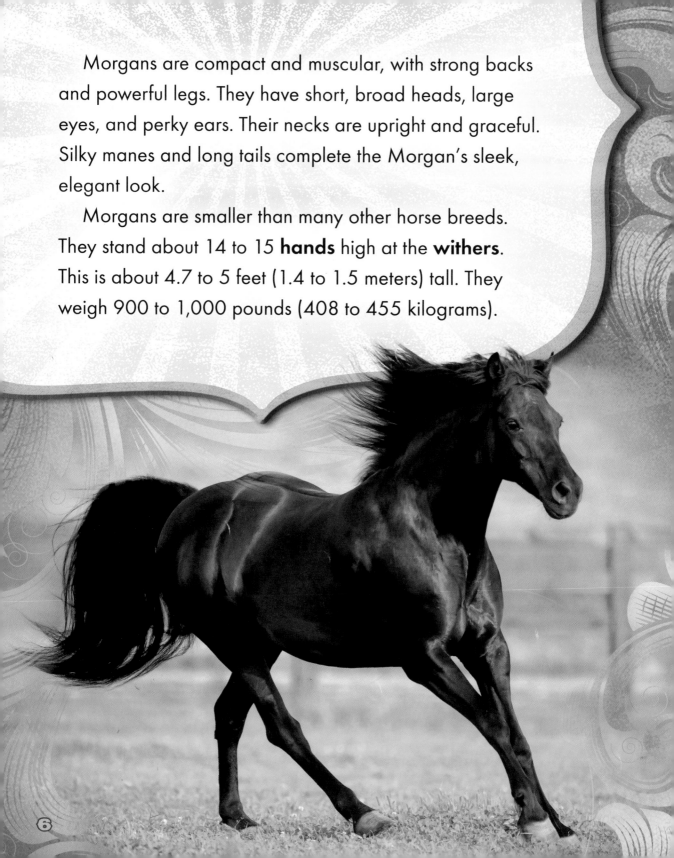

Morgans are compact and muscular, with strong backs and powerful legs. They have short, broad heads, large eyes, and perky ears. Their necks are upright and graceful. Silky manes and long tails complete the Morgan's sleek, elegant look.

Morgans are smaller than many other horse breeds. They stand about 14 to 15 **hands** high at the **withers**. This is about 4.7 to 5 feet (1.4 to 1.5 meters) tall. They weigh 900 to 1,000 pounds (408 to 455 kilograms).

buckskin

The Morgan's soft, shiny coat comes in many colors. The most common colors are bay, black, brown, and chestnut. Bay horses are reddish brown with black manes and tails. Chestnut coats are copper in color. Less common colors include palomino, dun, and buckskin. Palomino horses are tan with blond manes and tails. Duns are yellowish brown with a black stripe down the middle of their backs. Buckskins are tan with black manes and tails. Many Morgans also have white markings on their faces and legs.

An Original American Breed

The Morgan is one of the few original American horse breeds. The **foundation horse** of the Morgan breed was a bay **stallion** named Figure. He lived in Randolph, Vermont in the 1790s. Figure was a small horse with a slender body and a sleek coat. His owner was a man named Justin Morgan.

At first, people thought Figure was too small to do heavy work. He soon proved everybody wrong. Figure turned out to be stronger than many horses twice his size. He pulled heavy logs from forests, hauled wagons, and helped plow fields. Figure was also very fast. When challenged to race, he outran almost every other horse.

Unknown Origins

Definite information about Figure's parents is unknown. However, many believe that Figure's father was a Thoroughbred named True Briton. His mother probably had either Arabian or Friesian bloodlines.

Go Figure!

Justin Morgan loaned Figure to a man named Robert Evans. He needed a horse to pull logs from a forest. One evening after a long day's work, Figure and Evans were on their way home. They came upon some people standing near a large log. The log needed to be pulled to a nearby sawmill. None of their horses had the strength to do the job. Evans bet the group that Figure could pull the log. He was so confident about Figure's strength that he invited three large men to sit on the log. Much to the men's amazement, Figure pulled the log to the mill.

Figure quickly became famous around New England for his speed, strength, **endurance**, and gentle nature. Many people bred their **mares** with Figure. The **foals** grew up to have the physical traits of their father. In time, Justin Morgan sold Figure to new owners. People began to call Figure by his former owner's name, the Justin Morgan horse. They called his **descendants** Morgan horses. The Morgan horse is the only breed descended from one horse.

In the 1800s, the Morgan was one of the most popular breeds in New England. Morgans were known for being well-rounded horses. They helped clear logs from forests, pulled people in carriages, and worked on farms. **Harness racing** was becoming popular during this time. Morgans dominated this sport for many years.

A Powerful Figure

Figure's foals inherited more traits from him than from their mothers. Scientists call this special ability prepotency. Without this rare ability, the Morgan horse breed would not exist.

Morgans played an important role in the **American Civil War**. Soldiers in the **cavalry** often rode Morgans. They knew the horses could handle the hardships of war. Morgans had the strength and endurance to travel long distances without getting tired, even when food and water were scarce. On the battlefield, they were loyal and brave.

In 1909, Morgan owners from Vermont formed the Morgan Horse Club. To showcase the Morgan's talents, they invited all Morgan owners to bring their horses to the Vermont State Fair. Many people saw the breed for the first time. In 1971, the club's name changed to the American Morgan Horse Association (AMHA). The AMHA keeps track of Morgan **bloodlines**. To be **registered**, a foal must have two Morgan parents registered with the AMHA. Today, there are more than 145,000 Morgans registered with the AMHA.

Morgan Horse Farm

In 1907, the United States government started a Morgan breeding farm in Weybridge, Vermont. They bred stallions for use by the U.S. military until 1951. Today, the University of Vermont operates the Morgan Horse Farm. Visitors participate in educational programs and guided tours of the stables.

13

A Horse of Many Talents

Today's Morgans are as talented as their **ancestors**. They excel in a wide variety of events. One is called combined driving. One horse or a team of horses compete in this event. The horses are attached to carts with drivers. The carts have two or four wheels and often have elaborate designs. Drivers usually wear fancy hats and gloves.

Combined driving includes three separate rounds. The first tests the grace and style of the horses. The second is a long distance race that tests endurance and **agility**. This part of the course includes water, steep banks, and sharp turns. In the third round, horses maneuver carts through a tight obstacle course. The horses and their drivers are given penalty points if they make mistakes. The team with the fewest penalty points wins. Morgans have earned top honors in combined driving competitions all over the world.

Morgans also stand out in an action-packed event called **reining**. It tests the speed and endurance of horses. In reining, riders guide horses in different patterns, often at high speeds. One of the most difficult skills is the sliding stop. Horses use their hooves to skid on the ground before coming to a complete stop. Beginner horses only skid a short distance. Advanced horses can slide up to 20 feet (6 meters) before stopping!

Calling All Morgans

The Grand National & World Championship Morgan Horse Show is the biggest Morgan event of the year. This weeklong show is held every October in Oklahoma and draws over 5,000 spectators. Over 1,000 Morgans and their owners from across the United States and other countries compete for awards and prize money.

Morgans continue to work on ranches and farms all over the world. Their gentle nature also makes them popular riding horses for people of all ages and skill levels. Whether they are racing around an obstacle course, helping cowboys round up cattle, or carrying children on trails, Morgans can be counted on to perform their best.

The Blood of a Morgan

The success of Morgans has made their characteristics desirable to breeders. The horses have been bred into the bloodlines of the American Saddlebred, Tennessee Walking horse, Standardbred horse, and American Quarter horse.

Glossary

agility—the ability to move the body quickly and with ease

American Civil War—a war fought between the Northern states and the Southern states of the U.S. from 1861 to 1865

ancestors—family members who lived long ago

bloodlines—the family histories of horses

cavalry—military troops on horseback

combined driving—an event in which horses pull carts in three separate rounds; the three rounds are a dressage competition, a cross-country marathon, and an obstacle course.

cooperative—willing to work with others toward a common goal

descendants—animals that can be traced to a particular animal

endurance—the ability to do something for a long time

foals—young horses; foals are under one year old.

foundation horse—the first horse of a specific breed; all horses of a breed can trace their bloodlines back to the foundation horse.

hands—the units used to measure the height of a horse; one hand is equal to 4 inches (10.2 centimeters).

harness racing—an event in which a horse or group of horses pulls a cart and rider; a harness attaches the cart to the horses.

mares—adult female horses

registered—made record of; owners register their horses with official breed organizations.

reining—an event in which riders guide horses through a precise pattern of circles, spins, and stops

show ring—the ring where horses compete and are displayed at a horse show

stallion—an adult male horse that is used for breeding

temperament—personality or nature; the Morgan has an intelligent, calm temperament.

withers—the ridge between the shoulder blades of a horse

To Learn More

At the Library

Feld, Ellen F. *Blackjack: Dreaming of a Morgan Horse.* Goshen, Mass.: Willow Bend Pub., 2007.

Funston, Sylvia. *The Kids' Horse Book.* Toronto, Ont.: Maple Tree Press, 2004.

Henry, Marguerite. *Justin Morgan Had a Horse.* New York, N.Y.: Simon & Schuster Books for Young Readers, 2002.

On the Web

Learning more about Morgans is as easy as 1, 2, 3.

1. Go to www.factsurfer.com.

2. Enter "Morgans" into the search box.

3. Click the "Surf" button and you will see a list of related Web sites.

With factsurfer.com, finding more information is just a click away.

The images in this book are reproduced through the courtesy of: Sabine Stuewer / KimballStock, front cover, pp. 18-19; Sarah K. Andrew, pp. 4-5, 14-15, 16-17; Ryan Lasek, p. 6; Carol Walker / Minden Pictures, pp. 7, 10-11; blickwinkel / Alamy, pp. 8-9; Steve Apps / Alamy, pp. 12-13; Dusty Perin, pp. 20-21.